Portugal Celebrations and Holidays

Delfina Teixeira Tamulonis

By the same author:

A Practical Guide To Colloquial Portuguese
Vol. 1, *Conversando*

A Practical Guide To Colloquial Portuguese
Vol, 2, *Debate*

The Portuguese
Who Are We And Where
Are We Now?

Estrangeiros em Portugal

Published in Portugal by:
Delfina M. T. Tamulonis/Publicações Espiral
Apartado 463
2750, Cascais
Tel: (01) 482 7052; Fax. (01) 482 7053
e-mail: tamulonis@mail.telepac.pt

Dep. Legal: 124742/98
ISBN: 972-96802-5-6
        9 789729 680250

Printed and Bound in Portugal by
Uniprint, Cascais

Table of Contents

About the Author

Delfina Tamulonis is an author, publisher, language instructor/consultant and translator. A native from Portugal and a graduate from the University of Lisbon (Languages and Humanities), for many years she worked in Washington D.C. as a Portuguese instructor and translator. Currently she lives and works in Cascais, Portugal.

1

A National Bouquet

Flowers are part of our way of life. We do not leave a traditional market without a bunch of carnations, daisies, gladiolas or roses lying there on top of the potatoes, the fresh sardines, the finely chopped up kale (to make the soup *caldo verde*), the slices of pumpkin and all kinds of fruit. Fresh cut flowers are a mandatory detail in a Portuguese home along with olive oil, a bottle of Port, a selection of table wines and an Expresso coffeepot. We associate different varieties of flowers with distinct feelings and events. The very common, colorful dahlias and daisies grow abundantly in every garden and convey a comfortable aura of plain joy and contentment. The long-stemmed gladiolas add a touch of elegance to any room and the fragile camellia is a sad reminder of romantic albeit tragic love. The modest charm of the little bouquets of violets are as much part of the *Baixa de Lisboa* scenery as the flower vendors in Rossio and rua Augusta: women who come down from the old quaint Bairros with small aprons tightened around their waists, hands on their hips, loose tongues and lively disposition. Mums and chrysanthemums are definitely not a first choice when it comes to decorating your home or giving someone a present. Their strong, unpleasant smell may explain why a lot of people feel reluctant to bring these floral varieties into their homes, but there is another reason. These flowers bloom profusely in the fall, and are, therefore, traditionally used in the cemeteries on All-Saints-Day (November 1), a National Holiday dedicated to bereavement, to remembering our loved ones who are no longer among us.

Somewhere in this national bouquet there is the rose. The rose is probably our most favorite flower. Its sweet lingering scent, which exudes even from the dry faded petals, suggests peace, quiet enjoyment and the simple, yet priceless pleasures of life. Roses are first and foremost a symbol of love. They are given to wives, mothers, grandmothers, daughters and friends on their birthdays, special occasions or any "I love you" occasion. Red roses symbolize eternal love and make a good, common present from husbands to their wives. Light pink and yellow roses, a soothing reminder of youth and rosy dreams are given to young girls. The word for pink in Portuguese is *cor-de-rosa*, which means "color of the rose". And this word actually gives color and meaning to a few idiomatic expressions. *Cor-de-rosa* suggests idealism, brightness and positive thinking. The very common expression "*ver tudo cor-de-rosa*" to see everything pink" simply means to be too optimistic, to believe that only good things will come your way. To match the English expression "a rose garden" we have *um mar de rosas* ("a sea of roses"). *Um romance cor-de-rosa* is a romance novel or a love story, unrealistic and with a happy ending. Roses, like love, require a lot of care; they must be given the right nutrients and they must be pruned in a certain way and sprayed regularly. Roses are also a key element in on of the most well known stories among the Portuguese of all ages: "The Miracle of the Roses" (*O Milagre das Rosas*), supposedly performed by Queen Isabel (1269-1336).

The Miracle of the Roses

Queen Isabel came to Portugal at the age of twelve as the young bride of a Portuguese king, D. Dinis (reigned from 1279-1325), and she was destined to become the personification of virtue and sainthood. Her compassionate, generous nature made her a legend that has lasted to the present day. She took care of the sick and the hungry. She even protected and gave shelter to her husband's bastard children. She played a role in the political arena by resolving conflicts between her own home kingdom of Aragon and Portugal and by helping her husband iron out differences with his own subjects. Stories of her extreme kindness and miracles reached Rome and she was canonized by the Pope in 1625. *A Rainha Santa* is the patron saint of Coimbra where she retired (*Convento St^a Clara-O-Velho*) when her husband died. In this city, festivities take place in her honor every even-numbered year. The so-called *"Festas da Rainha Santa"* start on July 4 and last for a week.

The Miracle of the Roses is told to every small child in every elementary school and it goes like this: Queen Isabel used to leave the palace quite often to go and help the poor and sick, carrying money and bread hidden in the pleats of her big cape. She was so virtuous that she always tried to conceal her generosity. One day the king "caught" her and wanted to know what she was carrying hidden in her cape. Taken by surprise she simply replied " *Just roses, milord* ". The king did not believe her and insisted she show him. Since the queen owed her Lord and King obedience, she had no choice: she unfolded the pleats of her cape. However, to her surprise, instead of bread and money, beautiful roses started sliding down the soft velvet.

April 25

Red carnations became a symbol of freedom and liberation when on April 25, 1974, democracy was reinstated in Portugal. After almost half a century of dictatorship and thirteen years of colonial war on three fronts (Angola, Mozambique and Guiné-Bissau) a military coup overthrew the government of Marcelo Caetano, Salazar's successor. In the aftermath of the revolution, the communist party tried to establish here a pro-soviet regime. They were in control long enough to nationalize 60% of the economy, causing the most serious crisis in our recent history. The fight between leftist and moderate forces also led us to the

4

brink of civil war. Fortunately in the end everything was solved peacefully. The folks in the colonies were not so lucky, though. A hasty and irresponsible decolonisation forced half a million Portuguese to flee their homes and start over here in Portugal and other countries.

2

October 5: The Republic

It is hard to picture Rotunda (or *Praça Marquês de Pombal*) with anything other than buses, speeding taxis and other vehicles, careless pedestrians and the authoritarian Marquis himself standing high and proud against the green background of *Parque Eduardo VII*, looking sternly down *Av. da Liberdade* towards his masterpiece: the *Baixa*. This conglomerate of straight-lined streets, classic, elegantly understated buildings on the northern bank of the River Tejo was to be a sample and a paradigm of the new direction and ideals he dreamt for the new Portugal, where organization and planning would replace improvisation, where the rationalism and knowledge of the 18th century would finally illuminate the minds of the Portuguese. He hoped that the devastating earthquake of 1755 had shaken to the ground widely spread medieval beliefs and general ignorance, so that on its ruins, a modern society based on order, discipline and progress could be built.

Eighty five years ago, on October 5, 1910, the situation in *Praça Marquês de Pombal* could hardly be described with words like "order" and "discipline". Instead there was mass confusion, a lot of uncertainty and a new regime for the country in the making: it was the dawn of the Republican regime in Portugal. The revolutionary troops were barricaded in the Rotunda (*Praça Marquês de Pombal*), while the

forces loyal to the king were stationed in **Rossio.**
Many conspirators backed off when the operation was
already under way, which, along with other
developments, led the head of the revolution,
Almirante Reis, to commit suicide in anticipation of a
disastrous failure. In spite of this tragic loss, in the
morning of October 5, 1910, João Relvas and other
mentors of the Republican Party addressed the people
from the veranda of the City Hall (*Câmara Municipal*)
of Lisbon and proclaimed victory. The last king of
Portugal, D. Manuel II, and his family were on their
way to exile in England. In the provinces the new
regime was instituted with practically no resistance. It
was said at the time that the Republic had been
proclaimed in the provinces by telegraph.

Some symbolic measures were taken right
away: the flag became red and green (instead of white
and blue), the *escudo* replaced the *real*, *A Portuguesa*
was adopted as our national Anthem and the
Portuguese spelling was simplified. A pivotal issue in
the republican program was the family. The
revolutionaries advocated freedom for women and
legal protection for children.

Now, you may wonder: what prompted the
Portuguese people to overthrow the sole system of
government they had ever known since the birth of
this nation in 1143?

First of all it was not a sudden, unexpected
event. The republican movement had been gaining
support and some credibility for years and years.
There were republican organizations in every city in

8

Portugal as well as in the colonies. It should be noted here that Portugal had been benefiting from freedom of expression and association guaranteed by the Constitutional Monarchy established in 1822.

The republican propaganda focused on two guiding principles: patriotism and anti-clericalism. The monarchy and its allies (the church in general and the religious orders in particular) were blamed for every malaise that was eating away the very core of the Portuguese society: widespread corruption, the deplorable state of education, general backwardness and underdevelopment. The first big wave of patriotic fervor was triggered by the commemoration of the 300th anniversary of the death of Luís de Camões (our greatest national poet who died in 1580). This idea to make Luís de Camões a patriotic symbol came from the intellectual mind of Teófilo Braga, a professor of literature who was to become the first president of the provisional republican government. These patriotic feelings were further exacerbated after 1890, when England sent us an ultimatum: the Portuguese were to withdraw their troops from the African territories between Angola and Mozambique. To the casual foreign historian this may appear to be just another military issue. For the Portuguese of the late 1800s, however, it was not so. The African Project or as it was referred to the "Pink Map", had become an aspiration of people all across the political spectrum and had been embraced with a passion by the population in general. Thus, when King D. Carlos gave in to the English demands, he was accused of treason and even of conniving with the English royal family. Very naturally this general mood proved to be a fertile ground for the republican ideals to grow and thrive. The assassination of the king and the heir to the throne in 1908 constituted the last blow to a weakening regime, for, the monarch, in spite of his errors, had prestige in the army and was well liked as a person by a vast segment of the population.

The rich and powerful *Companhia de Jesus* (the Jesuits) were the favorite target of fierce republican attacks. They were accused of luring wealthy ladies into the church in order to take over their worldly possessions and of brainwashing the young generations in their schools. The principle of anti-clericalism or even anti-religion was not easily accepted in the provinces where religious feelings were deeply rooted. Nevertheless, the republicans stood by it and kept on pointing out the advantages of a secular society, advocating the separation of church and state. They also kept attacking the Jesuits, trying to alert the population for the harmful results of their education. In his writings Teófilo Braga classifies the education provided by the *Companhia de Jesus* as dehumanizing, for it destroys the personality of the individual, turning him into a passive instrument of saint obedience." He claims that this type of teaching " develops the faculty of the memory but cripples the intelligence".

Once in power the republicans did not waste any time dealing with the Church. Among other radical measures, all religious orders were expelled

(1910) and the teaching of the Christian doctrine was banned from the schools.

The First Republic

In 1911 a new Constitution was approved. The word that best describes the so-called **First Republic** (1910-1926) is instability. During this period there were eight Presidents and fifty cabinets. As bad as it may sound the situation was not really any worse than the one to which Portuguese had grown accustomed during the Monarchy. All this and a dangerous financial situation led to a **Military Dictatorship** (1926-33) and subsequently to the **Estado Novo**, ruled by the Constitution of 1933 and Salazar. According to historian José Hermano Saraiva, there were three determining factors that explain the longevity (39 years) of the *Estado Novo*: the political parties were outlawed, censorship and the strong personality of the leader himself.

The Second Republic

The Revolution (or military coup) of Abril 25, 1974, marks the beginning of the **Second Republic** and a new direction for Portugal. The colonial adventure was over. The last colonial Empire in the world came to an end as the five African Colonies (Angola, Mozambique, Guiné-Bissau, Cabo Verde and São Tomé e Príncipe) were granted independence. East Timor was invaded and annexed by Indonesia on

11

December 7, 1975. Hundreds of thousands of *Timorenses* have died so far fighting for their right to self-determination. Negotiations with the Indonesians and in the UN have failed to solve this problem in spite of the efforts and commitment of the current Portuguese government.

According to the new Constitution of 1976, the **President of the Republic** represents the Portuguese Republic and makes sure the democratic institutions work well. He is above any political party and is elected directly by the people for a five-year mandate. He may be elected for a second mandate. According to the electoral laws, the Parliament or **Assembleia da República** has a minimum of 230 representatives and a maximum of 235. The Prime-Minister is appointed by the President of the Republic, after consultations with the parties represented in the Parliament and taking in consideration the results of the legislative elections. The other members of the cabinet are nominated by the prime-minister and then appointed by the President. Currently, there are four main political parties in Portugal: the **PSD** (*Partido Social Democrata*), the **PS** (*Partido Socialista*), the **PP** (*Partido Popular*) and the **PC** (*Partido Comunista*). There many other small parties ironically designated as **PPs** (*Pequenos Partidos Portugueses*). In two parliamentary elections the PSD obtained an absolute majority. This allowed an unprecedented political stability which has been much appreciated by the Portuguese in general. The charismatic ex-leader of the PSD practically

12

demanded an absolute majority as the main condition to run this country. Although Cavaco Silva and his government were criticized for their policies in the last couple years of his second and last mandate, there is a general consensus that he did a lot for his country.

3

Colours, Smells and Tastes of November

November 1

The month of November does not start out on a very happy note. The first of November, or All-Saints Day, is dedicated to remembering our loved ones who are no longer with us. In cemeteries all over the country groups of people walk around slowly and silently while. The air fills up with the light, scratchy sound of dried up flowers as they are swept gently away and off the marble that covers the graves, and the strong scent of fresh cut white chrysanthemums (or mums), still wet with tears of morning dew. Chrysanthemums, namely the big, white variety, bloom abundantly in Portugal at this time of the year and are used, traditionally, to decorate graves on this day. The skinny, droopy petals, the dull green foliage and unpleasant smell combined with its association with grieving and sadness do not make this flower a favorite when it comes to brighten up your home or someone's day.

It was also on the first of November that, in 1755, Lisbon suffered the most devastating natural calamity of its entire history. On this fateful day, a strong earthquake and the fires that followed turned to rabble and ashes the heart of what was then one of the richest European cities. In the aftermath of the tragedy, 25, 000 people perished and 10,000 buildings collapsed. Many of these were churches that were packed with god-fearing poor folks attending All-Saints-Day services.

Chestnuts and Wine

But life goes on, and if there is something the Portuguese can do and like to do is to enjoy it, preferably outdoors, in good company, savoring mouth-watering foods, washed down with a good, local wine. Almost every month of the year offers an opportunity to do something different and November is no exception. In small towns, villages and even cities it is time to get ready for a *magusto*, the last picnic before the winter rains settle in. Groups of friends, school mates or families pack some sandwiches, a bottle of *jeropiga* (unfermented wine beverage), a bagful of good chestnuts and head for wooded area where they look for a suitable clearing. When they find it, everyone gets busy gathering dry pine needles, sticks and tree branches to start a nice big fire. You wait patiently until the wood has burned down to red-hot charcoal and then you toss in the chestnuts (*castanhas*) — after a cut has been made in each one of them or they may explode in your face! As the days get shorter and shorter at this time of the year, the chestnuts will be done just as the bright orange tones of the sunset start to rise behind the pine trees and the nippy, damp air suddenly moves in. I am sure that for most Portuguese adults, and especially those of us who grew up in the northern regions of the country, roasted chestnuts (*castanhas assadas*) bring back warm childhood memories of small cold fingers wrapped around this most favorite treat; of persistent efforts toward mastering the skill of cracking the skins open in such a way so that the delicious white meat would pop out easily and in one piece.

We have a very common idiomatic expression that means "to be very upset": "As upset as a turkey on Christmas Day" (*Chateado que nem um peru no Dia de Natal*). Well! The same goes for pigs in the month of November. They are slaughtered without mercy, (in many places it is even some sort of ritual), for it is necessary to secure supplies of meat and sausages that are essential in the preparation of hearty winter dishes, mainly stewed beans (*feijoada*) and Portuguese boiled dinner (*cozido à portuguesa*).

Saint Martin's Summer

By mid-November we should resign ourselves to the fact that the winter is just around the corner. Not quite. The middle of the month usually brings a few days of hot weather, or what we call Saint Martin's summer (*Verão de São Martinho*). Now you may ask: what does São Martinho have to do with this out of season heat wave? According to the legend, São Martinho was one of those knights that wondered throughout medieval Europe, always willing to help people in distress. On a very cold, rainy day of November, precisely on the 11th, he was riding through the woods somewhere in Portugal, with a woolen cape very snug around his body, when he encountered a poor, old man, almost naked and shivering in the freezing rain. Out of the goodness of his heart, São Martinho took off his cape, cleaved in two with his sword and gave half to the poor man. God was so pleased with this kind gesture that made the sun shine so warm that neither one of them needed anything on their backs. And from this moment on we have been blessed with a few summer days in the middle of November. This saint is also associated with wine tasting, although the reasons thereof seem to be purely coincidental. The crushed grapes have been fermenting since early October and it is now time to taste the new wine: "On St. Martin's day one goes the wine cellar to taste the wine" (*No dia de São Martinho vai-se à adega e prova-se o vinho*).

4

December 1: Restoration of Independence

A Vacant Throne

On the eve of December 1, 1640, Portugal was just one of the Iberian nations under the dominance of Spain. Filipe II of Spain had taken over Portugal in 1580 legally and with very little resistance, following a very dramatic set of circumstances. The human and material resources we needed to sustain our Empire of the East were wearing thin and we were losing ground on the trade of the spices due to growing, fierce competition with other emerging sea powers. After a short-lived golden era, Portugal was impoverished again and decadent. To make matters worse, our young King, D. Sebastião, driven by foolish patriotic ambitions to revive the grandeur and prestige of this country, led himself an expedition to North Africa that turned out to be the most disastrous defeat ever inflicted upon this country. When it was all over half of the 17,000 combatants (5000 of them were foreign mercenaries) lay dead in the battlefield of Alcácer Quibir, in Morocco. Among them there was the 24-year-old king himself. As his body was never found, though, rumors started to spread that he had not died and would come back someday on a foggy morning riding a white horse to save Portugal.

With a vacant throne (the king did not have any heirs) and lacking the ransom money for the release of the many noblemen and soldiers that had been taken prisoner, Portugal was in a desperate situation, indeed. This feeling of helplessness that at the same time harbors a secret hope for a miracle, for some event or person that will solve one's problems is known as *sebastianismo* and is considered one of the Portuguese traits.

The Iberian Union: a Dual Monarchy

Filipe II, the powerful king of Spain and the grandson of a Portuguese monarch (D. Manuel I), was a legitimate pretender to the throne, but he was not the only one. He was determined, though, not to miss this opportunity to unify the Iberian Peninsula. And instead of using military force, he launched a very shrewd and ultimately successful diplomatic campaign to convince the Portuguese that the Iberian Union was the best solution. He managed to get the support of the ruling classes (the nobility, the bourgeoisie and the clergy), which came as no surprise, for the nobility was particularly afraid of popular revolts and therefore, very keen to accept the protection of such a powerful monarch. On the other hand, merchants and tradesman were lured by the possibility to move freely in the rich South American regions. Plus the upper classes had very close, cultural ties with Spain and the Portuguese court was even bilingual. Most of the Portuguese writers of the time wrote both in Castilian and Portuguese. In fact, Portuguese was considered the language of the people. The people or the "little folks" (*arraia miúda*) as they were called, were totally opposed to the Iberian Union.   When the Spanish troops finally invaded Portugal in June of 1580 (after Filipe II had been declared King of Portugal by the five Portuguese "governors") about seven thousand last minute *arraia miúda* soldiers made a last attempt to fight them, but were rapidly defeated.

Portugal and Spain were not supposed to be just one country, but rather a dual monarchy. Filipe II made a lot of promises (including keeping the autonomy of the country and the Portuguese as the official language, reform the administration and finances that were in total disarray and ensure political tolerance) and he kept most of them.

Regaining Independence

Filipe II (Filipe I of Portugal) was an excellent administrator and under his rule this country prospered. His successors, however, were not as popular which helped rekindle latent feelings of independence. And after sixty years of foreign rule, the Portuguese had had enough. The population in general was particularly concerned about the way Spain seemed to be neglecting our overseas possessions, namely Brazil, the most precious jewel in the crown. Thus, on the morning of December 1, 1640, a group of about one hundred noblemen set out to restore the "real" legitimate royal line, by giving the throne to Catarina de Bragança's grandson, D. João. After a swift, well-planned and orderly coup Portugal was again a free nation. Two weeks later, D. João de Bragança was acclaimed King of Portugal.

But Spain was not prepared to give up the dream of a Unified Peninsula that easily. We had to go to war and it was not until 28 years later that a peace treaty was signed, whereby Spain recognized Portugal's independence. The Portuguese victory in what is called the Restoration War would have been very difficult to attain had it not been for the English Military Alliance. To seal this alliance and as it was customary at the time, a Portuguese princess (D. Catarina de Bragança) married the English king, Charles II. Her dowry was nothing less than two important cities: Bombay, in India and Tangier in North Africa. Unhappy and childless, the princess returned to Portugal thirty-two years later after her husband died. She is mostly known for having introduced the tea drinking habit in the English court and in New York City she is remembered and honored in the borough that was named after her: Queens.

5

Spring Celebrations: Easter

Next to the rich Portuguese literary culture made up of famous novels and poems duly signed by their renowned authors, there are the folk tales, a collection of centenary stories and legends that have been passed on from generation to generation. Some stories may have been woven around people who lived so long ago that their names are totally forgotten. There are legends that relate to old houses, monuments, landmarks, fountains and even stones and rocks. These tales illustrate moral principles, values and wisdom that comes from experience. There is always a clear message about love, human sin or weakness. They also have three features in common: the characters have no names, the time and place are unknown or very vague and they always start with "Once upon a time   "(*Era uma vez....*)

Once Upon a Time

From Algarve comes one of the most beautiful, famous legends, a story that is reminiscent of the historic past of this region, a time (8-13th century), when Islam and Christianity coexisted there. Once upon a time there was a Moorish prince who married a beautiful Nordic princess. As happy as she was with her prince in her new, warm surroundings in Algarve, she could not help feeling homesick from time to time, mainly in the wintertime. She missed the snow that covered the mountains in her native land. It broke the prince's heart to see these shadows of sadness that set on his wife's face and he decided to do everything possible to wipe her tears. She opened up her heart to the prince and told him about this longing she felt for her country in the month of February; how at this time of the year, back home, she would look out the window and enjoy the beautiful sight of the snow covered mountains against the blue skies. As powerful as the prince was in his kingdom, he could not give the princess this particular present. To change the climate of Algarve was something beyond his power. He was determined, however, to find a substitute for all this whiteness his wife missed so much. And then, suddenly, he had an idea: why not use Algarve' endemic flora to create an illusion, to find a way to dress up nature in white at this time of the year? According to the legend this is how the almond tree groves became part of the landscape in this southern province. These days, the beautiful sight of the almond blossoms in February draws a great number of Portuguese and foreign tourists to this most southern part of the country.

Almonds are also an essential ingredient in the preparation of many of our traditional desserts and cakes: almond cake, a whole variety of almond cookies and the famous Algarve sweets, made of marzipan (almond paste and sugar) and shaped into different kinds of fruit (bananas, apples, pears, etc,) and colored. Any Portuguese kid associates almonds with Easter, mainly candied almonds, although the younger generation seems to be keener on the chocolate eggs and bunnies. At this time of the years you see a round sweet bread with one or more eggs on top in supermarkets and pastry shops everywhere. That is called *folar* and is traditional all over the country.

Fertility Rituals

The egg symbolizes fertility and life renewal. In fact, Eastern celebrations are a combination of pagan rituals of fertility and life and nature renewal that go back to immemorial times and the more modern Christian dogma of death and resurrection. We still find in some regions of Portugal traditional practices of symbolic fertility and mating games, where young men and women meet in the hills and woods and play erotic (usually innocent) games. In Minho, north of Portugal, the cult of certain rocks as having attributes that increase fertility and procreation still go on. Some of these rocks are shaped like an egg or a shell. In some instances peasants dig inside of them to build little chapels, a symbolic gesture of the regeneration of life: human life going back inside the egg, the womb, to be born again.

Unlike Christmas there is not a particular dish that we enjoy on Easter Sunday. Nevertheless, people seem to feast on some kind of meat, usually baby goat or roast suckling pig, as in the old days Christians were supposed to refrain from eating meat during Lent. People used to eat fried vegetables in a batter during this fasting period, a habit that was introduced in Japan by the Portuguese Jesuit priests in the 16th century.

If you wish to get acquainted and the feel the traditional religious practices, you will have to go the deep Portugal, to a village or small town, away from the big urban centers, where the Church bells still ring when someone is christened, gets married or dies and a procession never goes by unnoticed.

In the big cities like Lisbon, each parish has its own celebrations, but they are not s visible as in the provinces.

The Holy Week

The Holy Week starts on Palm Sunday (*Domingo de Ramos*) when people go to mass with a little bunch made of an olive tree branch and aromatic wild herbs like rosemary. Traditionally after the service the children give the bunch to their godparents and receive a little gift in return, called a *folar*. On Thursday evening a service is held in most churches, usually at 6:30, which is supposed to be an enactment of the Last Supper (*Última Ceia*) with the washing of the feet (*lava-pés*). That night the churches are open and lit for anyone who may want to drop in for a minute or two. In small towns it is customary to visit them all. On Holy Friday a procession is held, representing of the suffering of Christ (Jesus carrying the cross), St. Magdalene, the Virgin Mary and the casket. Many people gather along the streets holding lit candles silently while others watch from the windows, from which silk bedspreads (usually red) hang down. In Lisbon, the main procession leaves at 8:00 pm from the *Convento dos Paulistas*, near Largo de Camões and it is called the Burial Procession (*Procissão do Enterro*). In most villages all over Portugal it is customary for the priest to visit every single home on Sunday or Monday. The streets are swept, houses are given a good spring-cleaning and the outdoor steps are embellished with flowers to receive Christ on the Cross. A white linen tablecloth is spread on a small table in the front room and an envelope with a donation to the Parish is laid on top. Not long ago most people would just leave a bowl of dry beans or half a dozen eggs, that were swiftly grabbed by diligent priest's helpers and dropped in the bags they carried from home to home. Leaving money was a sign of affluence very few people could afford to display. But times have changed!

6

Summer Festivities

"The Popular Saints": June 13, 24 and 29

The poppies and daisies have withered and died in the meadows; the grass is beginning to turn brown under the scorching sun and flower-lovers keep the sprinklers running for hours in a desperate attempt to prevent the beautiful multi-colored petals from shriveling and giving in to the dry heat. As soon as the sun sets on the ocean, the refreshing Atlantic breeze moves in, cooling the hot summer nights and sweeping away the dust and pollution. Summertime is here and the Portuguese are on the move. Many are planning a holiday somewhere at the seaside, a few go abroad and a large number can't wait to leave the big city for their home villages, family farms and small towns, nestled in beautiful valleys and mountains all over Portugal. Going back to your birthplace (*a terra*) is a way of life in this country. The appeal of one's roots, of the native land is a dominant characteristic of the Portuguese. And the favorite time of the year to satisfy this deeply felt longing is, of course, the summer. This is the time of the year when the weather allows you to enjoy a relaxing walk through the cornfields and woods, a swim in the river or a picnic with relatives and childhood friends. Many make sure to be there for the *festa*, an yearly celebration of the village, town or city that attracts its own children residing in the big cities or abroad as well as people from nearby villages.

If you take a trip through the "deep" Portugal, off the main roads, you will not only discover ancient villages and lovely countryside, but you may also be forced to stop to let a procession or marching band go by. At dusk, you may have to beep your way through a lively crowd, chatting and dancing under paper decorations and fancy arches.... Most of these festivities evolve around a saint, the patron of the village and go back centuries, probably stemming from a compromise between ancient pagan celebrations and catholic fervor.

Santo António de Lisboa

St° António de Lisboa, the most popular Portuguese saint, was a Franciscan born and raised near the Cathedral in Lisbon in the 1200s. He died in Padua at the age of forty. Every year on the night of the 12th of June, the inhabitants of Lisbon come out in the streets and squares to celebrate their saint: in the medieval alleys and quaint *pátios* of the old picturesque quarters of Lisbon, traditional Portuguese music and firecrackers blast away into the wee hours. The familiar, smoky aroma of the *chouriço assado* (barbecued Portuguese sausage) curls up in the clear air and around the colored balloons and decorated arches. The strong smell of the fresh grilled sardines is somewhat mitigated by the sweet aroma of the traditional potted basil (*manjericos*) and the mild scent of carnations in full bloom peeking down from ancient balconies, through the intricate designs of the forged iron. This is the night of the year when people of all ages and walks of life come out in the streets to join the *arraial*. With the sole, healthy purpose of having a good time, they take their time to enjoy the simple, basic, uncomplicated and cheap pleasures of a way of life, which, we, the Portuguese, seem determined to preserve. Simple delights like savoring grilled sardines, *chouriço*, kale soup (*caldo verde*) served in clay pots, cornbread (*brôa*), olives), — all washed down with red wine (*vinho tinto*), lively chat, joke telling, a good laugh and a lot of dancing.

The *Marchas* of Lisbon

The *marchas de Lisboa*, initiated in 1932, have become since then a favorite trait of the celebrations of Stº António. A parade of groups of men and women representing almost every *bairro* in Lisbon, wearing colorful costumes and dancing/marching down Av. da Liberdade to an original song (*marcha*), compete for a prize. Municipal officials support this tradition, as it is viewed as a good way to encourage the residents of the different quarters of Lisbon to study their own history and customs. Thus, watching the parade you may recall the rural Benfica, the *fado* singers (*fadistas*) of Mouraria, the Madragoa of the fishermen, the distinguished look of Castelo, the factory workers and "charcoal girls" of Alcântara.

In Porto the celebrations are in honor of S. João and take place on the night of the 23th of June. There are bonfires everywhere and it is traditional to jump over them. The *arrais* go on all night. The favorite food is roasted young lamb; and to go with it a glass of *vinho verde* is a must, of course.

In Évora the festivities start on the night of the 28th June in honor of S. Pedro and continue on for a couple of days with a craftsfair.

June 10: Day of Portugal, Camões and Portuguese Communities Everywhere

Portuguese Outside of Portugal

One summer day I was visiting a friend in her new apartment in Cascais, enjoying a wonderful view of the ocean and feeling the cool breeze that at this time of the year always rises from the Atlantic late afternoon, sweeps the air clean and then wails through the night. We both graduated from the University of Lisbon (albeit totally different departments) and went in opposite directions: I was off to America and she drove her mini to Paris to further her studies and subsequently to other European capitals.

As we were chatting away I noticed a small black and white photograph on her desk: a little girl with a big smile in a summer dress. I picked it up and turned it around. In the back it read: Clarinha, Goa, 1961. I knew she had lived in India as a child, where her father, an officer in the Portuguese army, had been posted. I remember other childhood friends who left for Brazil, America, Mozambique, Angola, South Africa, wherever a large Empire, the hope for a prosperous future or dreams of making it in a big country took their fathers. Of the 14 million Portuguese born in Portugal, 4 million live abroad.

There are large Portuguese communities in France, Germany, Luxembourg, Switzerland, South Africa, United States, Canada, Venezuela and of course, Brazil. Wherever the Portuguese settle, as they adapt easily and quickly to new ways, they also build a little Portugal. On Ferry St. in Newark, New Jersey, Portuguese immigrants find everything their souls and habits long for: codfish, *chouriço*, collards, kale, every newspaper (from *A Bola* to *O Expresso*) all kinds of pastries, music, etc.

On the 10th of June, our most important national holiday, we celebrate not only the spirit of Camões, but also Portugal, its unique culture and universal values and the Portuguese communities everywhere. These days one talks a lot about *portuguesismo* (of which the Portuguese language is the main aspect), a concept that does not just involve the Portuguese influence in other lusophone countries. It is also the cultural, natural interchange — not imposed by any agreements formally signed by politicians, which allows for people here, in Portugal, to dance to African or Brazilian music, or for an Angolan *fado* singer to pour out the same sounds and feelings of her best Portuguese counterparts. Like one of the most respectable Portuguese politicians, Prof. Adriano Moreira, said once in a television program, "Portugal is not in Europe, it is not in Africa, Portugal is in the world."

Some of the most prominent Portuguese writers and poets found their creative genius somewhere in this "world" and away from Portugal. Camões wrote his "*Os Lusíadas*" in India and Eça de Queirós, the widely read nineteenth century novelist — writing from London — did not spare his blows of irony on the Portuguese and the bourgeois society of the time. José Rodrigues Miguéis (1901-1980), whose sensitive, beautiful prose delights many Portuguese, lived most of his life in New York City.

Other outstanding, internationally known literary figures needed to be here, in close contact with the culture, the people and the land. Fernando Pessoa, (1888-1935) our greatest poet after Camões, was raised in South Africa and at the age of 18 decided to return to his roots in Lisbon, where his genius flourished. The great poet and writer Miguel Torga (1907-95) says in the last volume of his Diary: "I could never be a Portuguese writer outside of Portugal. Away from Portugal I would lack the language of the land, the grammar of the landscape and the Holy Spirit of the People".

We chose the date of Camões' death to celebrate the Portuguese nation not just because he is our most admired poet and an internationally known literary figure. Not even because he wrote so beautifully about this land, its people and their extraordinary deeds in his long epic poem, *Os Lusíadas* (published in 1572), which places Portugueses literature among the worlds greatest.

The major reason is because Luís de Camões stands for ideals, dreams, a philosophy and a way of life with which we have identified throughout our long, unique history. The so-called "spirit of Camões" is nothing less than the spirit of universality, of love of one's homeland, of struggle and survival against all odds. It entails the conviction that this nation will never die. It also has to do with those traits that seem to be so Portuguese: that blend of idealism and pragmatism, the adaptability to new cultures, the tendency to be citizens of the world, the appeal of the Atlantic and the longing, the *saudade* that brings us back home.

Throughout the centuries, it was that pragmatism that allowed us, a small, poor country at the edge of Europe, to built empire after empire in three continents. This pragmatism, however, always appears entwined with an idealism, which nourished the dream, until 1974, of a lusophone Atlantic Triangle (Portugal, Brazil, Africa).

Os Lusíadas

In his superb epic poem, *Os Lusíadas*, Luís de Camões tells us about the determination of one man, Vasco da Gama, to accomplish what he had set out to do when he sailed from Restelo (Lisbon) in 1497: to reach India by sea. And he did it. And in doing so, he showed "new worlds to the world" (*novos mundos ao mundo*). This extraordinary event changed the course of human history and made the world as we know it.

But *Os Lusíadas*, our literary masterpiece, is not just about the discovery of the maritime route to India. The voyage of Vasco da Gama becomes a symbol of the struggles, tribulations and peaks of glory of this Iberian nation, "on the most Western point of Europe" (*no ponto mais ocidental da Europa*), "where the land ends and the sea begins" (*onde a terra se acaba e o mar começa*).

Vasco da Gama battled against tides, threatening waves, contrary winds, traitors, hostile natives and fear — in the same way the Portuguese have fought hard and long for their independence (mainly against our powerful neighbor), obstinately trying to establish their place in Europe and in the world they discovered.

The life of the great poet itself can be an illustration of the history of Portugal, the Portuguese spirit, the spirit of Camões.

Luís de Camões

An impoverished nobleman, born around 1527, Luís de Camões studied in Coimbra and did his military service in North Africa where he lost his right eye. Later, back in Lisbon he was thrown in jail following a scuffle in the streets of the capital. After a year he was pardoned and soon after left for India in the service of the Empire.

He arrived in Goa in 1553. During his many years in the East, Camões was a warrior and a poet, "always holding the sword in one hand and he feather in the other" (*numa mão sempre a espada e noutra a pena*). He fought pirates, survived a shipwreck off the coast of China, wrote beautiful lyrics and his famous epic poem *Os Lusíadas*. Finally, in 1570 and after sixteeen years of wandering in the East, tired and broke, he manages to make it home, "to this garden planted by the seaside" (*a este jardim à beira-mar plantado*) thanks to the generosity of a friend who pays his way from Mozambique to Lisbon. In 1572 he fulfils a dream of a lifetime: his precious epic poem, *Os Lusíadas*, was published in Portugal and enthusiastically praised by the King himself who awarded the poet a small pension.

Luís de Camões died in 1580, poor and heartbroken "with his homeland" (*morro com a Pátria*), as he watched the collapse of the Portuguese Empire of the East, and his beloved country (*ditosa Pátria minha amada*) fell under the dominance of Spain. *Os Lusíadas* is not just about Portugal and the Portuguese. Its universal, timeless message has to do with the tenacity of the human spirit, with struggle and accomplishment, fear and courage, with venturing into the unknown. Both in his lyrics and epic poem, Camões reflects on man's perilous search for power, riches and glory (*Ó glória de mandar ó vâ cobiça*), on his solitary journey through life, disappointments, "mistakes, bad luck, passionate love" (*erros meus, má fortuna, amor ardente*) and self-affirmation, reason and passion (*amor é um fogo que arde sem se ver/É ferida que dói e não se sente/É um contentamento descontente*), quest for love (*Para mim bastava amor somente*) how short life really is (*E a nossa vida escassa /Foge tão apressada/Que quando começa logo é acabada)* and inevitable change (*Mudam-os tempos/Mudam-se as vontades).*

The Winds of Change

Change is definitely the keyword in Portugal today. We have been changing dramatically for the past thirty years. In spite of Salazar's attempts to keep the traditional values of modesty, patriotism and Christian principles in general, even before the revolution in 1974, the country was unstoppably on the move, socially and economically. Economical and social development and the rise in the standard of living are very visible all over Portugal. Statistics do not lie. In 1974 life expectancy was 69.9; today it is 73.6. In 1970 only 47% of the homes had running water, 58% had sewage and 63 electricity, today those numbers are 89%, 91% and 98% respectively. Infant mortality was reduced from 39% in 1970 down to 11% in 1991. The revolution in education is outstanding: 1n 1960 the school population was 1,140 000; today it is 2,290,000. We have not accomplished all this by ourselves, though. Europe is standing right behind us with her money in exchange for loyalty. After being an Atlantic nation for over 400 years, we are back in Europe where we are supposed to take our place, quietly and discreetly in a community of nations. We are told what to do and when and how to do it. Or in another words, when Brussels tell us to jump we simply reply "How high?" Almost everything comes from the EU these days: money, apples, potatoes (while we bury our own) and toxic waste. Our agriculture is in a shambles. Desperate farmers are selling off their ancestral family farms to real estate companies that turn them into golf courses. Europeans enjoy our sun and pleasant weather a lot more than they need our fruit and vegetables. We were told to forget about Africa and turn to sophisticated European markets. The only problem is that historic and cultural ties can not be severed by decrees imposed by eurocrats in the European Commission or by costly economic advice. The Portuguese can not forget about Africa. The tragedy of Angola and Mozambique is a national, deep wound that will take a long time to heal.

Portugal: What Future?

As we enter a new millenium, there are vital issues that concern us as an ancient nation, disturbing occurrences that leave us baffled. Are we bowing too much to European interests? Many Portuguese turn the other way when they see the blue flag with white stars flying over almost every road being built or historic building that is being renovated.

As Europe pumps millions into Portugal, many of us wonder whether this will really contribute to a general, sustained development of the country or whether they are nothing but a third version Indian and Brazilian riches, which benefited only a few and left the country poor.

Generations from now, will these Euro funds be visible only in the concrete of the highways and beautiful bridges? Would the tons of gold from Brazil be buried in a few palaces and monuments such as the Palace of Queluz and the Monastery of Mafra? Will we be able to remain an independent nation, a nation with a free will and a unique culture? Camões died poor "with his homeland" in 1580. Now, at the end of this millenium is Portugal dying rich?